Natural Disasters

Teaching Tips

Turquoise Level 7

This book focuses on the grapheme **/a/**.

Before Reading

- Discuss the title. Ask readers what they think the book will be about. Have them support their answer.
- Ask readers to sort the words on page 3. Read the words together. Reinforce that /a/ can have a short /a/ sound or a long /a/ sound.

Read the Book

- Encourage readers to read independently, either aloud or silently to themselves.
- Prompt readers to break down unfamiliar words into units of sound and string the sounds together to form the words. Then, ask them to look for context clues to see if they can figure out what these words mean. Discuss new vocabulary to confirm meaning.
- Urge readers to point out when the focused phonics grapheme appears in the text. Does it have a short /a/ sound or a long /a/ sound?

After Reading

- Ask readers comprehension questions about the book. What kinds of natural disasters were explained in the book? Have you experienced any of these?
- Encourage readers to think of other words with the /a/ grapheme. On a separate sheet of paper, have them write the words into two columns: one under the short /a/ sound and the other under the long /a/ sound.

5357 Penn Avenue South
Minneapolis, MN 55419
www.jumplibrary.com

Decodables by Jump! are published by Jump! Library.

Library of Congress Cataloging-in-Publication Data is available at www.loc.gov or upon request from the publisher.

ISBN: 979-8-88996-879-5 (hardcover)
ISBN: 979-8-88996-880-1 (paperback)
ISBN: 979-8-88996-881-8 (ebook)

Photo Credits
Images are courtesy of Shutterstock.com. With thanks to Getty Images, Thinkstock Photo and iStockphoto. Cover – IgorZh. 4–5 – arzmadani, John D Sirlin. 6–7 – Felix Mizioznikov, Vladislav Gurfinkel. 8–9 – Jewelzz, MyImages – Micha. 10–11 – mrizag, NayaDadara. 12–13 – Christian Vinces, Youkonton. 14–15 – 4.murat, Microgen. 16 – Shutterstock.

Can you sort these words into two groups? One group has **a** as in **mat**. One group has **a** as in **bagel**.

apricot

lady

cat

catch

bacon

last

angel

plaster

We live on an amazing planet. From parks to plains to wetlands, there are all sorts of sights to see. Fantastic people, plants, and animals are found across the globe.

However, there can sometimes be frightening events that happen on this planet. What happens when the rain will not stop? What happens when the land beneath us falls apart?

On some days, you might feel a lot of wind outside. However, a hurricane is much more frightening. A hurricane is a swirl of wind that can destroy whatever stands in its path.

Hurricanes start out at sea. The winds swirl around and gain speed as they get closer to land. As they hit the land, they may pass over towns.

Hurricane winds are so fast that they will not just rip a branch off a tree. They will rip up the entire tree!

You must stay safe if a hurricane is on its way. Do not wander in the street or stand and watch. You must get to a safe shelter.

Disaster can strike when you least expect it. Sometimes, the ground is not as safe as we think it is.

A landslide is when part of a hill or cliff drops away. When this happens near a town, it can squash things underneath it, such as homes.

The part of our planet under the ground is made of rock. When that rock shifts under the sea, it can make a colossal wave.

If the wave lasts until it meets the land, it can destroy all that lies in its path. The waves can be so vast that entire towns can be washed away.

Each time a disaster happens, lots of people come to help the people affected. Experts might go to help people repair their homes.

It is important to look after people, as disasters can affect us all. We need to make sure that help is there when they happen.

Say the name of each object below. Is the "a" in each a long /a/ sound or a short /a/ sound?

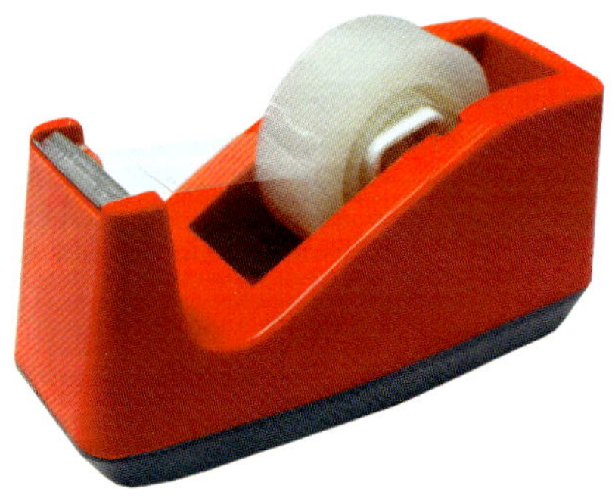